ROBOT BASICS

WORLD BOOK

www.worldbook.com

Co-published by agreement between Shi Tu Hui and World Book, Inc.

Shi Tu Hui
Room 1807, Block 1,
#3 West Dawang Road
Chaoyang District, Beijing 100025
P.R. China

World Book, Inc.
180 North LaSalle Street
Suite 900
Chicago, Illinois 60601
USA

© 2026. All rights reserved. This volume may not be reproduced in whole or in part in any form without prior written permission from the publisher.

WORLD BOOK and the GLOBE DEVICE are registered trademarks or trademarks of World Book, Inc.

Library of Congress Control Number: 2025938160

Robots
ISBN: 978-0-7166-5814-6 (set, hard cover)

Robot Basics
ISBN: 978-0-7166-5815-3 (hard cover)

Also available as:
ISBN: 978-0-7166-5825-2 (soft cover)
ISBN: 978-0-7166-5835-1 (e-book)

WORLD BOOK STAFF

Writer: William D. Adams

Editorial

Vice President
Tom Evans

Senior Manager, New Content
Jeff De La Rosa

Associate Manager, New Content
William D. Adams

Content Creator
Elizabeth Huyck

Proofreader
Nathalie Strassheim

Graphics and Design

Senior Visual Communications Designer
Melanie Bender

Photo Editor
Rosalia Bledsoe

ACKNOWLEDGMENTS

Cover: © 35lab/Shutterstock; © WowWee Group Limited; Borba Zal (licensed under CC BY-SA 4.0); © Tertill Corporation
4-5 © Well Photo/Shutterstock; NASA/JPL-Caltech/MSSS
6-7 © Jenson/Shutterstock
10-11 © Magicin Foto/Shutterstock
12-13 © Macroact Inc
14-15 NASA/JPL-Caltech; © marekuliasz/Shutterstock; © asharkyu/Shutterstock
16-17 © Science Photo/Shutterstock
18-19 NASA/JPL-Caltech/MSSS
20-21 © Robomow Friendly House
22-23 Public Domain
24-25 © Vandamm Studio/Alamy Images; Eureka Entertainment
26-27 © Ralph Crane, The LIFE Picture Collection/Getty Images
28-29 National Institute of Standards and Technology; © Asharkyu/Shutterstock
30-31 Borba Zal (licensed under CC BY-SA 4.0); © FANUC
32-33 © Meen Na/Bigstock; © Alesia Kan, Shutterstock
34-35 © WowWee Group Limited; © Paul Hilton, Bloomberg/Getty Images
36-37 © Chris James, University of Glasgow; © Ned Snowman, Shutterstock; © J. Tal, Shutterstock
38-39 © Tertill Corporation
40-41 NASA/JPL-Caltech
42-43 © Saildrone, Inc.
44-45 © Chris Bardgett, Alamy Images; © Miriam Doerr Martin Frommherz, Shutterstock
46-47 © For Inspiration and Recognition of Science and Technology (FIRST); © Cloudy Design/Shutterstock; © tdee photo cm/Shutterstock

Contents

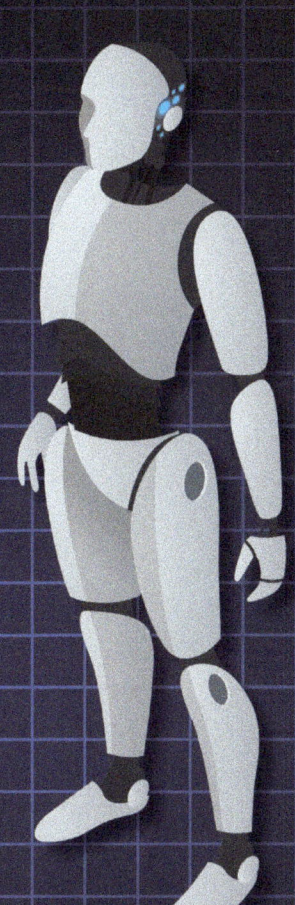

- **4** Introduction
- **6** What Is a Robot?
- **8** What Does a Robot Look Like?
- **10** Humanoid Robots
- **12** Sensors
- **14** Actuators and Power
- **16** Computer Brain
- **18** A SPA for Robots? Sense-Plan-Act
- **20** ROBOT CHALLENGE: Let's Go with Plan B
- **22** Life Before Robots
- **24** Imagining Robots
- **26** Robots Come to Life
- **28** Industrial Robots
- **30** HELLO, MY NAME IS: LR Mate 200iD
- **32** Toy Robots
- **34** HELLO, MY NAME IS: Robosapien X
- **36** Robot Helpers
- **38** HELLO, MY NAME IS: Tertill
- **40** Robot Explorers
- **42** HELLO, MY NAME IS: Saildrone
- **44** Robots of the Future
- **46** Hands-On Robotics
- **48** Glossary and Index

Terms defined in the glossary are in type **that looks like this** on their first appearance on any spread (two facing pages).

introduction

Robots are all around you, even though you might not know it. They work in many factories, creating the products you use every day. Robots explore the deepest oceans and farthest reaches of space, gathering data for scientific discoveries. You can spot them counting items on grocery store shelves, helping out around the house, and watching traffic. Soon they may drive us around.

Robots are great at doing dull, dirty, and dangerous work. A robot can perform simple, repetitive tasks all day long, much faster than a person could.

From ordinary...
Robots can perform the same simple task over and over again without complaint.

…to extraordinary
Robots explore places where people cannot safely go, such as the surface of Mars.

Robots don't get grossed out or sick from dirty working conditions. And they can work in places where it isn't safe for people to go. As engineers improve robotics technology, robots will do more of these kinds of jobs, leaving more time for people to do more interesting—and fun—things.

In this book, you will discover what makes a robot a robot. You will read a little about robot history. You will learn about where robots can be found and the different jobs they can do. You will also meet some real-life robots and find out about their abilities.

What is a Robot?

These industrial robots are programmed to automatically weld automobiles.

This is a book about robots. But just what exactly is a robot? What makes a robot different from a computer or a power tool? A robot is a **programmable** machine that can perform actions automatically to accomplish a particular goal. Let's break that down a bit further:

- A robot is *programmable* in that people tell it what to do through computer language called code.

- A robot is a *machine* because it operates in the physical world. Many computer programs can perform actions to work towards a goal, but they do so in the digital realm.

- A robot performs at least some actions *automatically,* without help from a person. This automatic performance of actions is called **autonomy.**

- A robot performs actions in order to accomplish a particular goal set by its programmer. This may be as simple and well-defined as "put these two pieces together" or as complex and open-ended as "find and rescue trapped survivors."

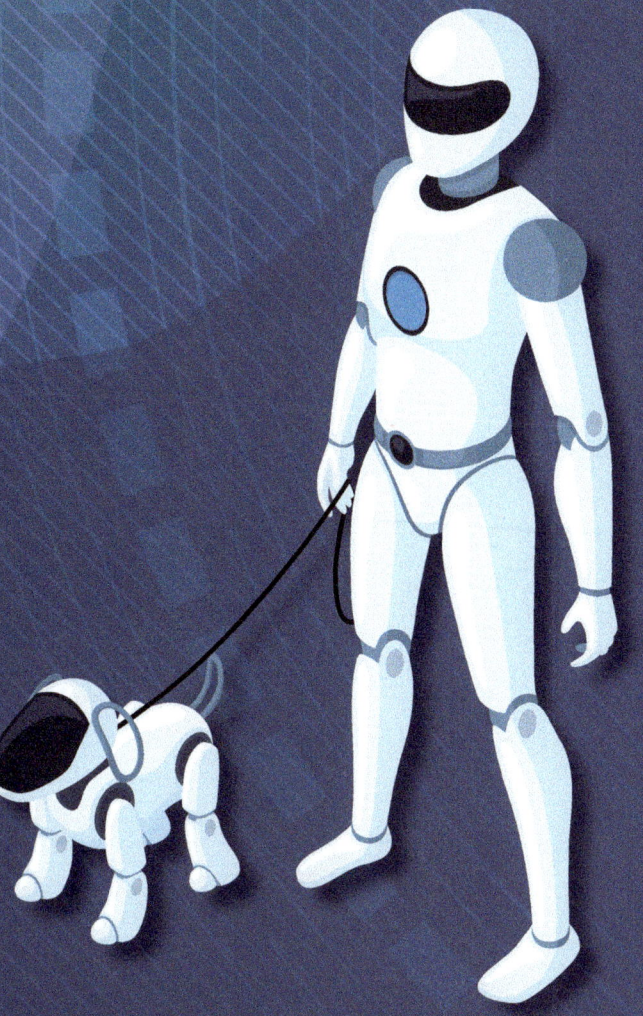

What Does a Robot Look Like?

The kind of body a robot has depends on the job it does. Robots can look like humans, animals, vehicles, or other machines—or have a shape all their own. Robots can be made to roll, walk, fly, swim, or stay in place. A robot can be as small as a cell or as large as a truck.

Many people think of complex **humanoid** machines when they hear the word "robot," but many robots are quite simple. Even traffic signals and washing machines can be thought of as robots! They are **programmable** machines that perform actions (such as change light colors, or add water and spin clothes) to accomplish a goal (making traffic flow smoothly or cleaning clothes).

Even though robots come in all shapes and sizes, all robots share certain features that allow them to sense and interact with their environments. In addition to some sort of body, all robots have **sensors, actuators,** and **effectors.**

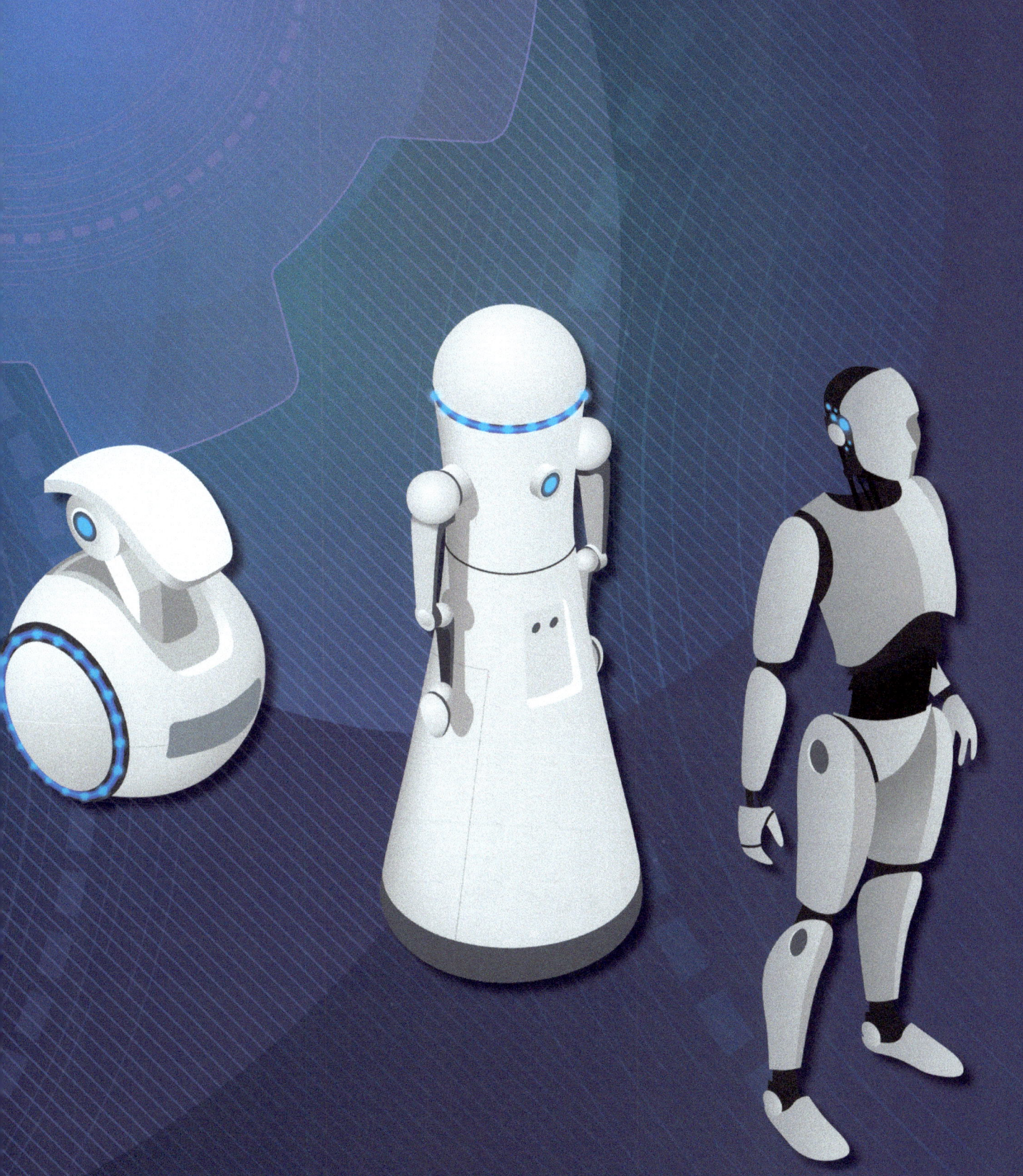

Humanoid Robots

Robots that have the general shape of a person are called **humanoid robots.** Inventors may create humanoid robots for many reasons. First, being shaped like a human allows the robot to work more easily in a human environment. Humanoid robots can move through buildings, open doors, and use hand tools. Second, a robot may be given a humanoid appearance so it is easier for humans to talk to or work with the robot. Third, engineers design humanoid robots to impress people. A humanoid robot looks a lot cooler than a simple **articulated robot!**

"How do you do?"
A child watches a presentation from a humanoid robot.

Sensors

A robot needs **sensors** for two things: detecting the state of parts of itself and detecting the state of the outside environment.

All robots must sense the status of at least some of their parts. For example, a robot might sense the angles of its arm joints or the positions of its wheels with sensors called encoders. A robot might keep track of the status of its internal systems, such as its temperature or power level, so it can act to keep itself in working order. A robot might also need to sense how it's interacting with the outside world. For example, it might find out how tightly it is gripping an object using force sensors.

All robots must also somehow measure their environment. For example, a robot might need to detect and identify objects that it needs to use or avoid. This information is often gathered through cameras and different types of sensors.

Touch sensor (center-head)

Proximity sensor

Lights

Camera

Speaker

Inertial sensor (senses the robot's own movement)

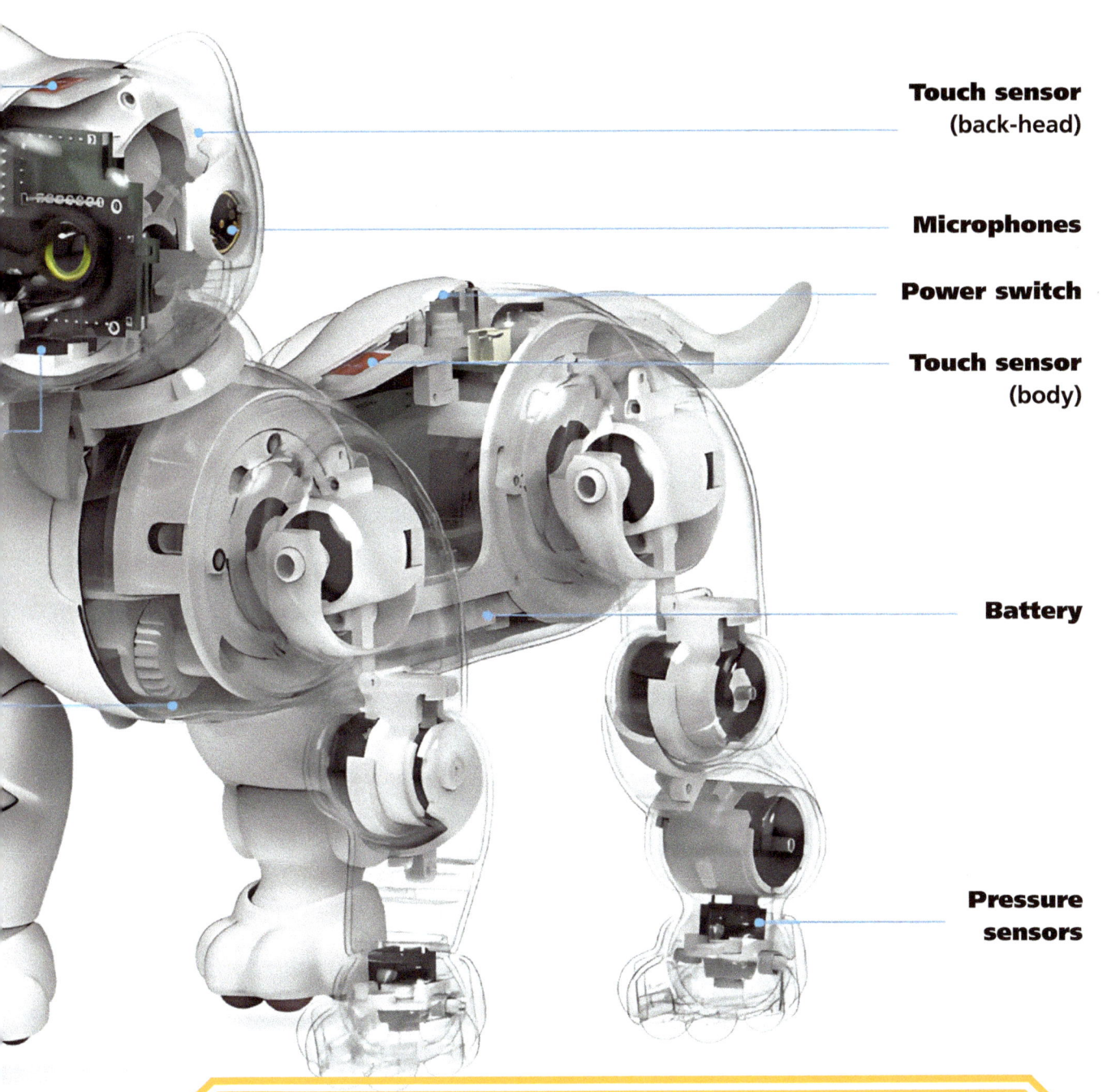

- Touch sensor (back-head)
- Microphones
- Power switch
- Touch sensor (body)
- Battery
- Pressure sensors

New sensation
Instead of muscles and nerves, this robot cat moves with motors and senses touch with pressure-sensitive plates in its head and body.

Actuators and Power

A robot moves with **actuators.** The most common actuators are motors. The part of the robot's body that the actuator moves is called an **effector.** An effector is a piece of a robot that interacts with the environment to perform an action. Wheels, propellers, arms, hands, and grippers are all effectors.

Without power, a robot is going nowhere fast! Robots that stay in place are simply plugged in to a power outlet. Robots that move around typically use batteries. As battery technology has improved, these robots work longer before needing to recharge. Some robots, such as many space probes, use solar panels to recharge their batteries.

It's great to actuate!
Effectors are parts that move and do tasks. Wheels, grips, and rotors are all effectors.

Computer Brain

At the center of every robot is a computer, its brainy **hardware.** Like the robot's body, its hardware is designed to best suit its job. A robot with many **actuators** designed to do complex tasks will need a powerful computer that can smoothly manage many processes at once. If a robot must go a long time without a charge, its hardware will be chosen to save power.

Robots are controlled by computer programs, or **software,** that give them goals and instructions. Almost all robots have software that can be reprogrammed for different tasks. This is important for **industrial robots,** which often have bodies that allow them to be adapted to many different kinds of work.

Computer hardware runs the software programs that direct a robot.

[16]

A SPA for Robots? Sense-Plan-Act

A robot can sense the outside world and the robot's own position in it, figure out what action needs to be taken to achieve a goal, and perform this action. This cycle of detection, decision, and action is often called *sense-plan-act*.

First, a robot gathers information with its **sensors.** It then feeds this information into its program to plan out how to accomplish its goal. Finally, a robot follows its plan to achieve its goal. This involves using **actuators** and **effectors** to change things in its environment or the robot's place in it.

Cycles of sense-plan-act happen all the time. The robot takes in new information, adjusts its plan if it has to, and acts on the adjusted plan. For instance, say a rover is traveling over ground that turns out to be sandy, causing some of the wheels to lose traction and spin a little. If the robot was simply counting wheel turns to figure out how far it needed to go, it might stop in the wrong place. But with continuous cycles of sense-plan-act, the rover can use cameras and other sensors to see that it has not moved as far as it predicted in the original plan, revise the plan to move forward for longer, and travel to its destination.

Sense-plan-act is an important cycle for the Mars rover Perseverance. The rover must detect and avoid rocks and pits as it **autonomously** navigates to a scientific target.

If you're making a sandwich and realize you're out of pickles, you can decide whether to make the sandwich without pickles or go to the store to buy some. But a robot might have a hard time figuring out what to do. It might keep looking in the fridge for pickles forever!

Autonomy is the degree to which a robot can make decisions without help from a human operator to achieve a goal. All robots have some autonomy, but some have more than others. And no robot is fully autonomous. All must have some help from a human operator—even if only in picking the robot's task.

Autonomy is useful, but it is hard to program. To keep things simple for **industrial robots,** engineers often place them in carefully designed **structured environments** that limit the number of unexpected things that can happen.

A robotic lawn mower can autonomously set out to cut grass, avoid obstacles, and return to base when it is raining.

But as robots move into everyday life, they will need greater autonomy. In unstructured environments, random events happen all the time. It's impossible to plan for everything. With the help of AI, new robots are learning to classify objects and events, learn from past experiences, and know when to ask a human for help.

Life Before Robots

For thousands of years, people have dreamed of creating versatile machines to do boring work for them. But it has only been possible to make real robots in the last 75 years. Technological breakthroughs that led to the creation of robots include **automation,** harnessing electricity, and the invention of **programmable** computers.

Many civilizations that discovered how to make things out of metal have created **automatons.** These figures, often shaped like people, contained many gears and springs that drove lifelike movements. Craftspeople created complex automatons that could write, draw, drink, and play musical instruments. But these automatons were powered by wind-up mechanisms or weights, which couldn't make enough energy to do much useful work. They also performed set routines and had no **autonomy.**

During the 1800's, inventors began thinking of ways to automate processes that took lots of time. Using steam power and electricity gave inventors ways to power large and complex machines. This led to huge changes in how things were made. But these machines still weren't robots.

Automatons, such as these three from the 1700's, could perform such tricks as writing, drawing, or playing music. They were a big hit at parties!

Imagining Robots

The later **automatons** of the 1800's were so complex that they seemed almost like living things. Combined with the rise of steam and electric power, they inspired writers to imagine what living machines might look like and how they might act. In the series of fantasy books by L. Frank Baum describing the land of Oz, the Tin Woodman and Tik-Tok were mechanical characters that today would be considered robots.

Robot uprising
In the play *R.U.R.*, automatons kill their human masters and take over the world.

In the film *Metropolis*, a mad scientist builds a robotic version of his long-lost love.

The word "robot" was first coined in the 1921 play *R.U.R.*, written by the Czech playwright Karel Capek *(KAR uhl CHAH pehk)*. "Robot" comes from a Czech word for "laborer." Portrayals of robots in books and movies exploded after *R.U.R.* In 1927, the German film *Metropolis* became the first major film to feature a **humanoid** robot. In 1940, American science fiction writer Isaac Asimov wrote the first of his *I, Robot* stories. These stories had a huge impact on how robots were viewed in science fiction and inspired future engineers.

Robots Come to Life

The first modern computers were created in the mid-1900's. They were electronic, rather than mechanical, so they were much smaller and didn't use a lot of energy. They were also **programmable,** meaning different **software** could be run on them.

In 1948 and 1949, American-born British scientist William Grey Walter created two of the first robots, often called "turtles" because of their rounded shells and slow movement. These robots moved toward light and changed direction when they bumped into something. Just by following these two simple rules, the turtles displayed lifelike behavior.

In 1967, engineers at Stanford University in the western U.S. state of California created Shakey, a robot that could make simple **autonomous** decisions. Shakey could be given general instructions to perform a task, such as picking up an object and moving it, and figure out the best way to accomplish that task. It worked in a highly **structured environment,** however.

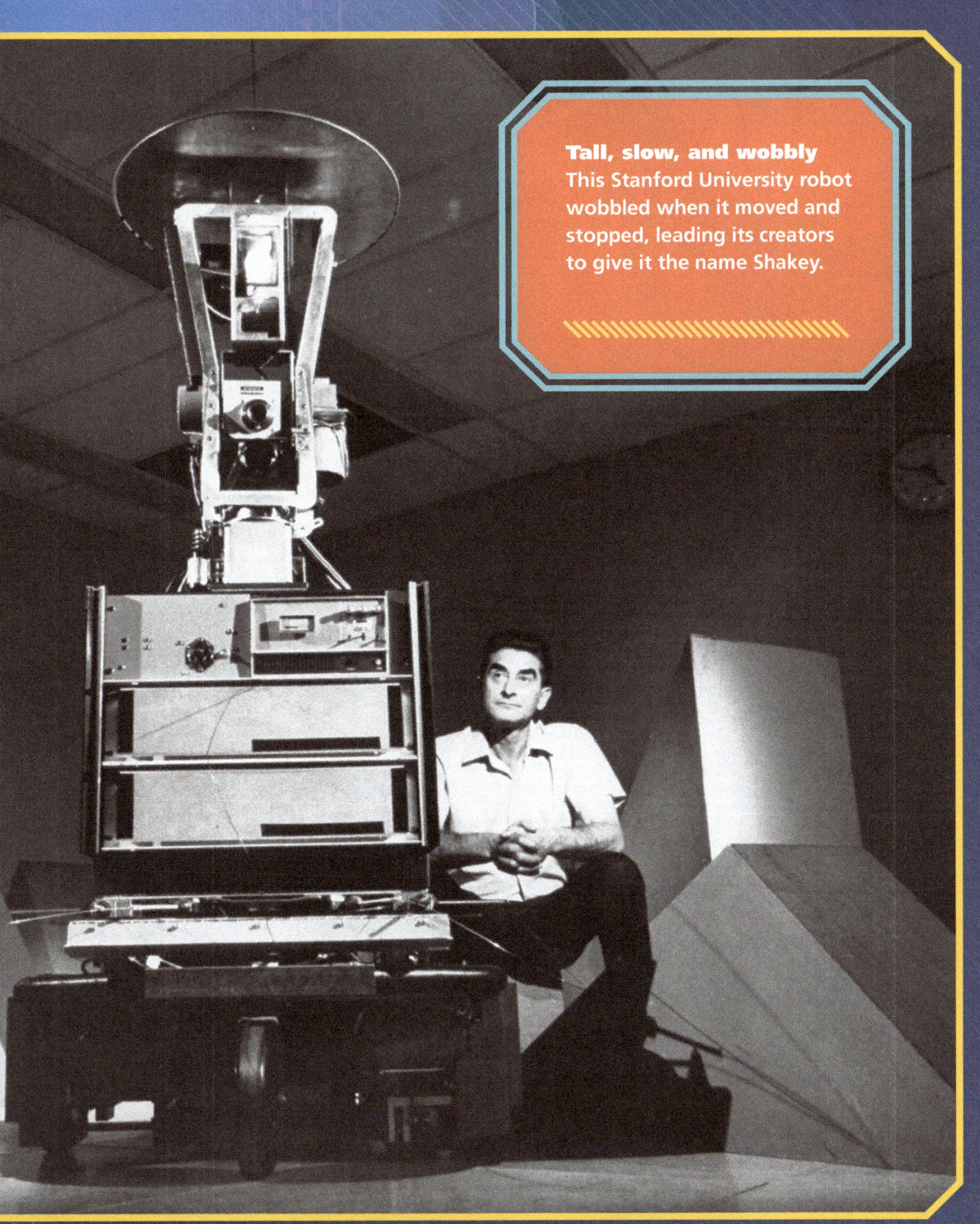

Tall, slow, and wobbly
This Stanford University robot wobbled when it moved and stopped, leading its creators to give it the name Shakey.

Industrial Robots

In the 1960's, robots made the jump from being scientific curiosities to useful workers. In 1961, the first **industrial robot**, Unimate, was added to the assembly line of an automobile manufacturing plant in the eastern U.S. state of New Jersey. Other factory managers soon saw the value of using robots to perform very precise and repeatable movements under dangerous

Wanted: Robots
In the early days of the industrial robot, the U.S. government set up the Automated Manufacturing Research Facility to experiment with new methods of robotic manufacturing.

Modern industrial robots come in all shapes and sizes. They can handle all kinds of tasks.

conditions. Robots quickly made their way into many kinds of factories.

Industrial robots can perform a huge variety of tasks and are designed to be flexible and efficient. The most common type of industrial robot is an **articulated robot** in the shape of an arm. Different **effectors**, such as grippers, welders, and paint sprayers, can be mounted at the end of the arm to fit the robot's task.

HELLO, MY NAME IS:

LR Mate 200iD

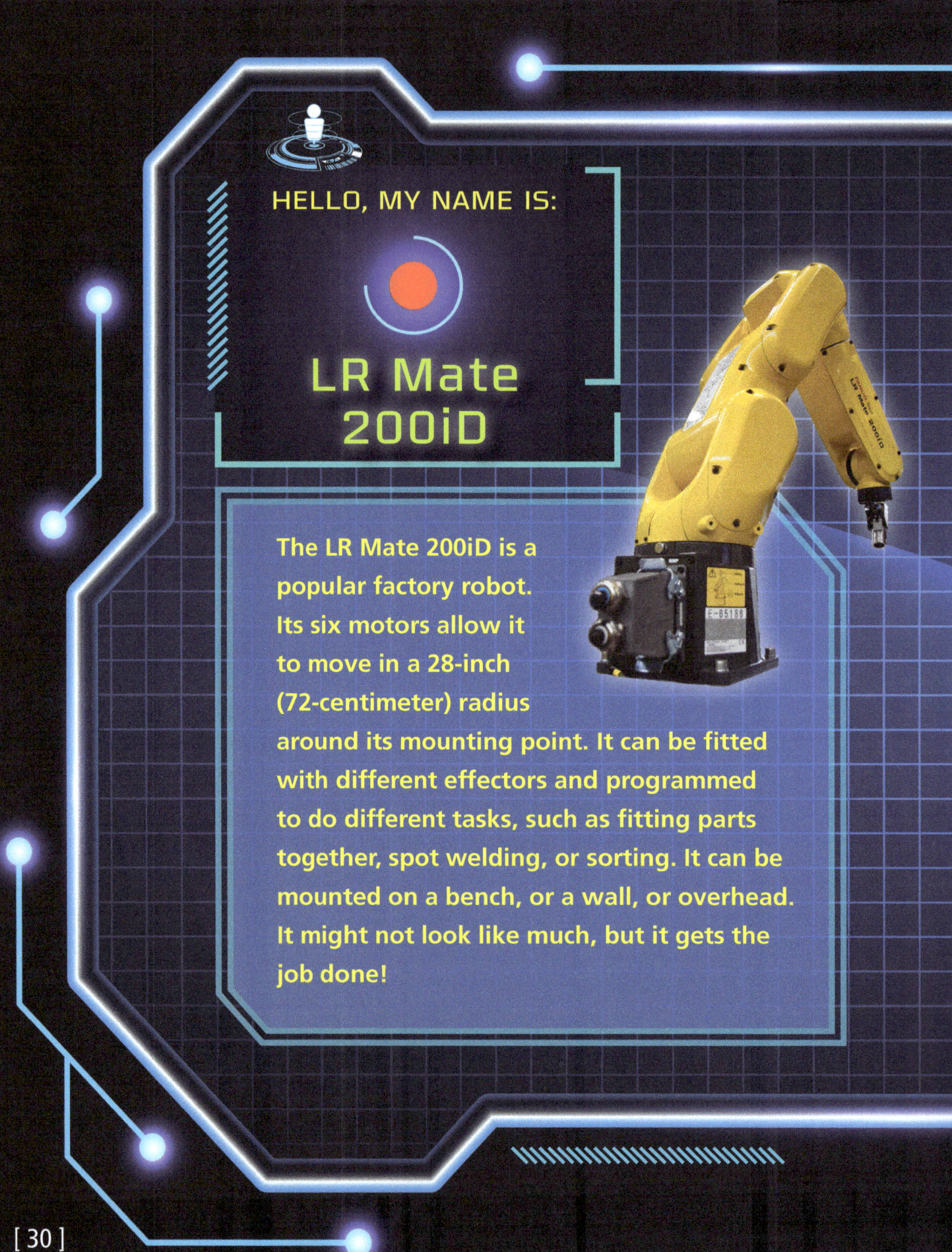

The LR Mate 200iD is a popular factory robot. Its six motors allow it to move in a 28-inch (72-centimeter) radius around its mounting point. It can be fitted with different effectors and programmed to do different tasks, such as fitting parts together, spot welding, or sorting. It can be mounted on a bench, or a wall, or overhead. It might not look like much, but it gets the job done!

AUTONOMY

`LOW`

The LR Mate 200iD can be programmed to handle some unexpected situations, but it usually needs human help if something out of the ordinary happens.

FLEXIBILITY

This robot is designed to help in all kinds of tasks. Versions of the LR Mate 200iD can be used to weld, move things, grind metal, or put parts together. It can even work with food!

FRIENDLINESS

It's just a giant yellow arm. It isn't designed to detect or interact with people, so stay clear.

MAKER

The LR Mate 200iD is made by the Japanese robotics company FANUC.

STRENGTH

LR Mate 200iD can lift up to 15 pounds (7 kilograms).

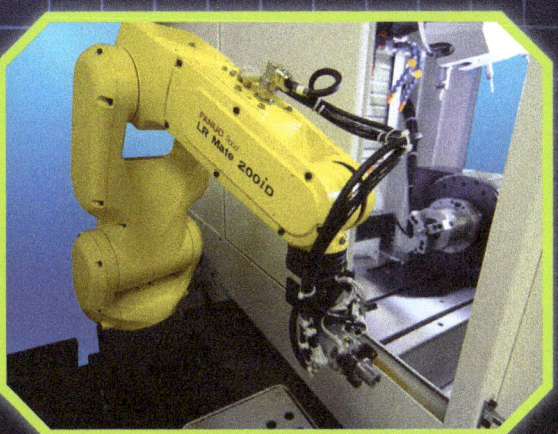

Toy Robots

Many robots entertain us as toys. **Automatons** have amused and amazed people for thousands of years. Egyptian rulers were sometimes buried with them. Until a few decades ago, limitations in robotics technology meant that most robots were simply curiosities. As technology has

Tin toy
Early robot-themed toys were not really robots at all, but they inspired a generation of scientists and inventors.

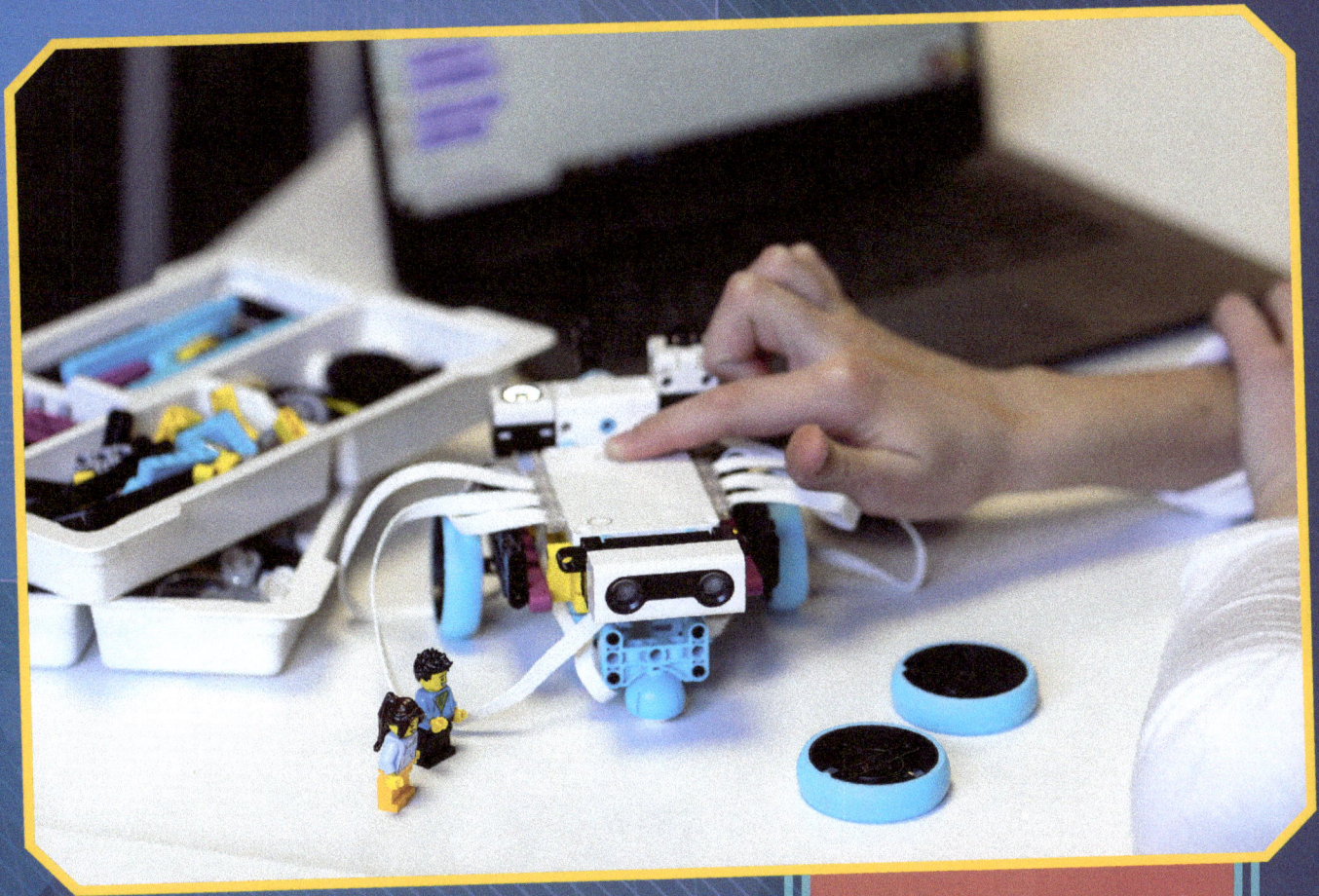

improved, people have made more complex robotic toys.

Playing with a robot can be fun, but designing and building your own robot can be even better! Robotics clubs help children, teens, and adults create and program their own robots. Such kits as LEGO Spike, VEX, and Makeblock let people build robots using simple building pieces and program them with a computer.

LEGO Spike kits enable people to build and program their own robots using LEGO bricks, sensors, motors, and a small computer "brick."

HELLO, MY NAME IS:

Robosapien X

Robosapien X is a toy robot for all ages. Kids enjoy directing the robot from its remote control and watching it dance. Tech-savvy teens and adults can program Robosapien X to do all kinds of things, such as guard the house, alert people to social media updates, or even play soccer!

AUTONOMY

LOW TO MEDIUM

In basic mode, Robosapien X can't do much on its own. It responds to sounds but is mostly remote-controlled with an app. But users can also program it to be more autonomous.

PERSONALITY

Robosapien X can whistle, do karate, and even dance!

MAKER

Robosapien X is made by the Hong Kong- based toymaker WowWee.

HEIGHT

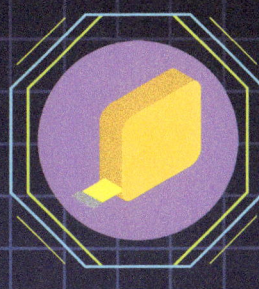

14 inches (35 centimeters)

Robot Helpers

Robots can now help out in more than just factories. In hotels, robots can act as front desk receptionists and bellhops. Some robots help in hospitals. Others serve as companions to elderly people in nursing homes.

'Bot guides
The University of Glasgow is working on a robotic guide dog for people who are blind. Its first job is taking visitors around a local museum.

Robots are also starting to help out around the house. Some clean floors and mow lawns. These tasks are pretty simple, so the robots only need a few **actuators.** Other robots serve as home assistants. They can monitor connected devices, turn on the lights, tell you the weather, take messages, and keep an eye on kids and pets. Future home bots may help tidy up rooms and do simple chores.

Robotic vacuum cleaners are common household robots. They can help ensure that you never come home to dirty floors.

HELLO, MY NAME IS:

Tertill

Gardening is fun, but no one likes pulling weeds. Why not have a robot do all the work while you sip lemonade and enjoy the flowers? The Tertill (pronounced "turtle") 'bot is designed to do just that.

This small solar-powered 'bot patrols between the plants, whacking down weeds with a spinning plastic string underneath and churning them up with its wheels. The wheels also help till the soil. It roams and recharges all day long.

AUTONOMY

MEDIUM

The Tertill patrols on its own, but the garden must have a short fence around its edge, and plant rows must be 12 inches (30.5 centimeters) apart. But the robot hunts weeds and recharges all on its own. It's even waterproof.

WEED ID

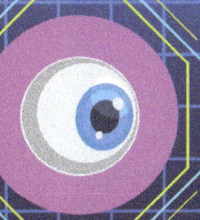

How does the Tertill know the difference between veggies and weeds? It assumes all tiny plants are weeds. If a plant is tall enough to touch its sides, it turns away. Gardeners can protect young plants with a metal bar.

SLOW AND STEADY

Tertill takes it slow, like a turtle. It weeds for a few minutes, then recharges for a bit, then weeds some more.

SIZE

2.5 pounds (1.1 kilograms), about as big around as a Frisbee

MAKER

Tertill is manufactured by Tertill, Inc.

Robot Explorers

Robots are far better at exploring new places than humans are. They don't need air, water, or food, just a power source. They can be designed to withstand a wide range of pressures and temperatures. We humans usually want to come back home when we're done exploring! A robot explorer can be left behind when its mission is over. For these reasons, robots have dominated space exploration. Humans have only made it as far as the moon, but probes and rovers explore every corner of our solar system.

Robots also excel at exploring areas of Earth that are dangerous to humans, such as the deep ocean and the Arctic and Antarctic regions.

Icy explorer
A scientist prepares a submarinelike robot to explore glacial waters in the U.S. state of Alaska.

HELLO, MY NAME IS:

Saildrone

If you want to collect data on conditions in the middle of the ocean, you could take a long, expensive trip on a research vessel, or anchor an instrument buoy to the seafloor. Both are expensive and take a lot of time. But a company called Saildrone Inc. has found a better way. They use fleets of autonomous sailing **drones** to gather data, which is used in weather prediction, climate modeling, and water testing.

Saildrones look a bit like a big orange surfboard with a stiff, narrow sail. The sail can turn to catch the wind, and also holds a solar panel. Larger models can handle long voyages in rough seas.

AUTONOMY

HIGH

Needing neither an outside fuel source nor human sailors, a Saildrone can sail around one spot or go on a data-finding cruise for months. If needed, humans can change the Saildrone's mission while it is out at sea. A drone only needs to return to port for maintenance and repairs.

PERSONALITY

A Saildrone looks more like a big surfboard with a sail than a robot. But it's easy to spot with that bright orange color scheme!

MAKER

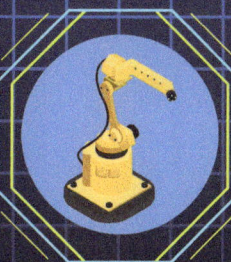

Saildrone Inc., based in San Francisco, California, builds Saildrones.

SEALS' SAVIOR

Cameras have shown seals clambering aboard the craft to rest or escape from sharks and killer whales!

SIZES

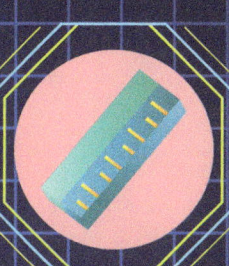

From 23 feet (7 meters) to 72 feet (22 meters) long

TOP SPEED

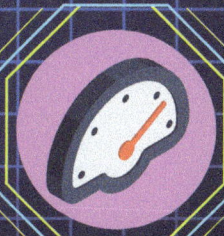

9 miles (15 kilometers) per hour

Robots of the Future

Robots have only just begun to change our world! With advances in programming and AI, robots of the future will be able to do more and learn on their own. That will help **industrial robots** become both more **autonomous** and safer for humans to work with. Self-driving vehicles are already in use in some cities. Soon they may become commonplace. Robots are also finding a place aiding doctors and working in laboratories. Other robotic advances might

Wall Butler
A smart home control panel can make your whole home into a robot! Connected to smart devices, it can turn on the lights when you get home, monitor deliveries, turn on music, and even start dinner.

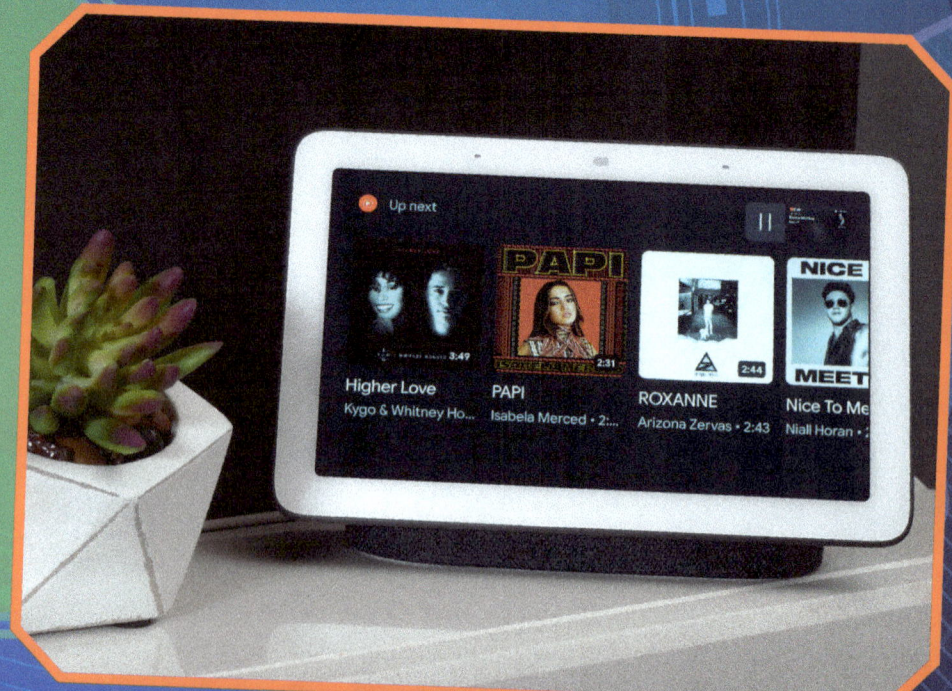

"This feline's shedding is increasing my sweeping duties by a factor of 4.65!" Future robots may be able to help out with more household chores.

come from the integration of computers and connected appliances. For instance, a smart home might figure out when no one is home and turn off the air conditioner to save energy. As robots continue to take on more dull, dirty, and dangerous jobs, humans will be free to spend more time performing rewarding tasks, coming up with new ideas, or just having fun!

Hands-On Robotics

Want to get started making robots? Jump right in!

FIRST Robotics

FIRST is a global robotics organization and competition with levels for younger, middle, and older kids. The first step is to form a team. Anyone can start one—it could be a school, community center, camp, religious organization, or just a group of friends. Each team builds and programs a robot to compete in a themed challenge, which changes every year. Teams also design logos and come up with an inventive solution to a real-world problem (such as cleaning rivers or helping wheelchairs climb stairs). FIRST emphasizes teamwork and "gracious professionalism," all teams helping and supporting each other. There are different levels of competition for different ages:

LEGO League (ages 4-16): builds robots from LEGO Spike bricks, motors, and **sensors,** and a **programmable** core.

Tech Challenge (ages 12-18): builds smaller robots (microwave-sized) out of any material.

Robotics Competition (ages 14-18): builds larger robots out of any material.

In the FIRST LEGO League, kids build robots from LEGO's to solve a common challenge. They also research a problem that robots might solve, design a team logo, and partner up with other teams.

Competitions are held at the local, state, national, and international levels, with winners advancing to the next level. Over half a million kids from 100 countries all over the world regularly compete.
And have a great time!

Also check out:
- VEX Robotics
- Best Robotics
- World Robot Olympiad
- National Robotics Challenge

Or ask about robot clubs or kits to check out at your local school, library, or maker space.

[47]

Glossary

actuator a device, such as a motor, that provides movement to a robot.

articulated robot a robot that uses rotary joints. The most common articulated robots are armlike industrial robots.

automation the use of machines to perform tasks that require decision making.

automaton a machine, usually shaped like a human or an animal, that performs lifelike actions. Automatons were usually powered by weights and springs and had no autonomy.

autonomy the degree to which a robot can make decisions without input from a human operator to achieve a goal.

drone an uncrewed aerial vehicle. Most drones are piloted remotely, but some are autonomous.

effector the part of the robot's body, such as a wheel or a gripper, that is moved by an actuator and interacts with the environment to perform an action.

hardware the physical parts of a computer.

humanoid shaped like or resembling a human.

industrial robot a robot that works in a factory to help create a product.

programmable able to be programmed.

sensor a device that takes in information from the outside world and translates it into code.

software a general term for computer programs. A computer program is mostly made up of a sequence of instructions. The instructions tell a computer what to do and how to do it.

structured environment in robotics, an area in which a robot operates that has been specially designed to reduce the number of unexpected occurrences while the robot is working. The flow of people, vehicles, and items not involved in the robot's task is usually restricted.

Index

A
actuators, 8, 14, 16, 18, 37
articulated robots, 11, 29-31
Asimov, Isaac, 25
automation, 22, 44
automatons, 22-24, 32
autonomy, 19, 31, 35, 39, 43; automatons and, 22; in early robots, 26; need for, 7, 21

B
batteries, 14
Baum, L. Frank, 24

C
Capek, Karel, 25
computers, 6-7, 22, 26, 44-45; in robots, 16-17

D
decision making. *See* autonomy

E
effectors, 8, 14-15, 18, 29
electric power, 14, 16, 24

F
FANUC (company), 31
FIRST, 46-47

H
hardware, 16
humanoid robots, 8, 10-11, 25

I
I, Robot stories (Asimov), 25
industrial robots, 6, 16, 21, 28-31, 44

L
lawn mower, 21
LEGO: League, 46-47; Spike, 33
LR Mate 200iD (robot), 30-31

M
Makeblock, 33
Metropolis (film), 25

O
ocean exploration, 40-43
Oz (fictional place), 24

P
Perseverance rover, 19
power, for robots, 14, 16, 24
programmable machines, 6-8, 22, 26

R
Robosapien X (robot), 34-35
robots, 4-5; appearance of, 8-9; as explorers, 5, 18-19, 40-43; as helpers, 36-39; autonomy in, 7, 21; definition of, 6-7; early, 26-27; future, 44-45; humanoid, 8, 10-11, 25; imagining, 24-25; industrial, 6, 16, 21, 28-31, 44; life before, 22-23; parts of, 12-19; sense-plan-act for, 18-19; toy, 32-35
rovers (spacecraft), 18-19
R.U.R. (film), 24-25

S
Saildrone (robot), 42-43
science fiction, 25
sense-plan-act (SPA), 18-19
sensors, 8, 12-13, 18
Shakey (robot), 26-27
smart home control, 44
software, 16, 26
space exploration, 5, 14, 18-19, 40
Stanford University, 26-27
structured environments, 21, 26

T
Tertill, 38-39
toy robots, 32-35

U
Unimate (robot), 28

V
vacuum cleaners, 37
VEX, 33, 47

W
Walter, William Grey, 26
WowWee (company), 35

www.ingramcontent.com/pod-product-compliance
Lightning Source LLC
Chambersburg PA
CBHW061253170426
43191CB00041B/2420